HERO DOGS

True Stories of Incredible Courage and Unconditional Love from Man's Best Friend

Lou Jefferson

Disclaimer

Disclaimer and Terms of Use: Effort has been made to ensure that the information in this book is accurate and complete. However, the author and the publisher do not warrant the accuracy of the information, text, and graphics contained within the book due to the rapidly changing nature of science, research, known and unknown facts, and internet. The author and the publisher do not hold any responsibility for errors, omissions, or contrary interpretation of the subject matter herein. This book is presented solely for motivational and informational purposes only

Contents

Introduction

Dogs and humans have been helping each other for generation after generation. In fact, there is now evidence that having dogs may have helped humans over 20,000 years ago to surpass the Neanderthals in the struggle to survive.

I've always loved having dogs and enjoyed their little quirks and how sensitive they have been to my own moods and wants. They seem to know when to sit and lean against your legs when you're working or when to grab the leash and plead for a walk.

Recently I read *War Hero: The Unlikely Story of A Stray Dog, An American Soldier and the Battle of Their Lives* by Stephan Talty. This book touched my heart and led me to read about the other amazing dogs in the world.

There are reams of stories about dogs saving dogs, dogs saving people, and dogs saving other animals. One of my favorites is China's Saihu. A mother dog with pups was attracted to the smell of cooking meat. The cook threw down some scraps of raw meat to the dogs but Saihu kept her pups away and wouldn't eat the meat herself. This continued until the cook went to serve the meat to a crowd of people. Saihu jumped forth, ate the scraps, and died quickly. Saihu's death stopped people from eating; giving time for someone to realize the meat may have been bad. It turned out that the meat was poisoned. Saihu saved not only her own pups but many people as well.

There are the several well-known types of dogs, from service dogs, to guard and sentry dogs, seeing-eye dogs, hearing dogs and war dogs. Dogs have been found to detect cancer by smell; it's hoped that by detecting the aromatic compounds the dogs smell will lead to improved early diagnosis with technological inventions – not bringing dogs to clinics.

Other dogs have been known for their extreme faithfulness ... refusing to budge from gravesites or from the last place they saw their human companion.

Then there are the mini-heroic actions of our own dogs. My favorite story came from a friend of mine. Like most mothers, his had taken over the training of Smitty from her kids and husband. One time, the family had to be away for several days. Back then, no one used boarding kennels in their small city. They made Smitty comfortable in the cellar. Providing plenty of dry food and water. They left papers over the dirt floor, assuming since he'd been paper-trained as a pup, he'd know what to do. Not Smitty. He was the mother's dog. When the family returned home and let Smitty outside – he *peed* forever – refusing to dirty mother's clean dirt cellar floor.

I picked the stories in this book to show both the dogs and their humans. I hope you enjoy reading them.

Lou

Balto and Seppala

Balto's story takes place around Nome, Alaska, in the winter of 1925. Winter in that area means living mostly in the dark and cold. In January, the sun rises around noon and sets before five. The winter of 1925 was the coldest one in 20 years: during January the temperatures dipped to minus 60 and even minus 70 degrees Fahrenheit. These temperatures cause frostbite in minutes if the skin is exposed to the air.

During the 1900-1909 Alaska gold rush, the population of Nome had grown to 20,000. But people left town shortly afterwards. By 1925, there were only 455 Alaska natives and 975 settlers from Canada, the United States, and Europe still living in the Nome area.

Diphtheria Outbreak

There was one doctor, four nurses, and a small hospital in Nome. In December, 1924, Doctor Curtis Welch treated a small girl for what he thought was a simple sore throat. She died the next day but the family wouldn't let the doctor examine her so he didn't know what disease she had.

In January, 1925, Billy Barnett, a three-year-old became sick. This time, Doctor Welch saw a thick patch at the back of Billy's throat and knew that Billy had diphtheria.

What's diphtheria? This is a disease caused by bacteria, those very small organisms that you need a microscope to see. The diphtheria bacteria squirt out a poison, called a toxin, which can cause fever and very sore throats. In some cases, the poison causes a gray leathery patch to grow in the back of the throat that makes it hard to breathe.

Many people died from diphtheria back then, especially children. Today we are given a vaccine so we don't get diphtheria. It's part of the DPT shots against diphtheria, pertussis (whooping cough), and tetanus given to children. Back then the vaccine was just being developed and not accessible to the general public. The only treatment was serum containing antitoxin which could help people fight the disease.

In Nome, when Billy was diagnosed with diphtheria, the antitoxin that Dr. Welch had on hand was too old and he was afraid to use it. The doctor had ordered new serum the summer of 1924 but it hadn't arrived by ship before Nome was iced in for the winter. Billy died the next day.

The day Billy died another child became ill. Dr. Welch tried the old serum but it didn't work and she died. He then radioed for help. He needed new serum, a lot of it. Diphtheria travels through the air easily and he was afraid everyone in Nome would get the disease. The town started that day to quarantine anyone with the disease, and one of the nurses was assigned to make sure sick people didn't come into contact with others.

By January 24, there were 20 new cases and 50 possible cases.

Serum was located in Anchorage, enough to treat 30 children. But how could they get it to Nome fast enough? There were no roads. The ocean was frozen so ships couldn't come in. The only two airplanes in town were open cockpit biplanes with water-cooled engines – so they weren't used in winter. The town usually got mail from Nenana, a port with open water in the winter. The mail was taken by dogsled to Nome, a distance of 674 miles. A normal mail run took 25 days.

Plan "A" and Plan "B"

Plan "A", the first plan they came up with, was that the serum would be sent by train to Nenana, the end of the line. Then two of the fastest sled dog teams would be used. One team would go from Nenana to Nulato, about half-way between Nenana and Nome. The other team would start from Nome, drive to Nulato, get the serum from the first team, and return with it to Nome. This second team had to be the best, and the best team in the area was Leonhard Seppala, the musher, and his dog team led by Togo, a Siberian husky.

Seppala had come to Alaska from Norway during the gold rush and stayed to work for a gold-mining company. He first used dogs to pull wheeled carts, mostly just for fun. But, living in Alaska, he got interested having dogs to pull sleds over the snow. Finally he joined others in the sport of dogsled racing.

In 1913, Seppala was training some dogs for Roald Amundsen, the famous explorer, for an expedition to the South Pole. But that trip was cancelled and Seppala was given the dogs. This was his first dog team. One of those dogs, Togo, was his favorite. By 1925, Togo was still his lead racing dog despite being 12 years old, which is rather old for such a rigorous sport.

Another reason for picking Seppala was that the most dangerous part of the journey was crossing Norton Sound. If Seppala used this shortcut both coming and going it would save a whole day in getting the serum to

Nome. Norton Sound had many perils. The winds can be fierce enough to topple the sleds. The ice can be smoothed by the winds such that the dogs have trouble even walking on it. Other times, winds and underlying sea currents can push the ice up into jagged piles, making it difficult to find a way through. Seppala had crossed Norton Sound several times. Any other musher would be more at risk of losing sled, dogs, serum, and his own life by attempting it.

So Seppala set out from Nome to Nulato with Togo and his other dogs. Right after Seppala left, however, people changed their minds about Plan "A" and went to Plan "B".

In Plan "B", many mushers and teams would start from roadhouses along the trail and relay the serum to Nome. With this plan, each dog team would go about 30 miles. They figured that Plan "A" was too much to ask of any team or musher.

The teams had scheduled rest stops in between their final stops to both rest and melt the serum. The 20-pound box of serum arrived in Nenana and was picked up by "Wild Bill" Shannon, who wrapped it in a quilt and headed out. He arrived at his first rest stop with his face blackened by frostbite in the minus 50-degree air and with three of his nine dogs too weak to continue. Two of the dogs died right there. When Shannon got to his next stop, they had to pour hot water over his hands to release them from the sled.

Meanwhile, as the relay team was progressing, Seppala had come 170 miles from Nome, crossing Norton Sound without difficulty. He was thinking he had much further to go, when he saw Ivanoff, a musher coming from the other direction. Ivanoff was part of the serum relay. Ivanoff had a rookie dog team that had run off the trail into a reindeer and his dogs and the sled were all tangled up in a mess. He was trying to fix it when he recognized Seppala's dog team passing a little way off.

Seppala had seen Ivanoff, but didn't know he had the serum. He was bent upon reaching Nulato to get the serum and didn't want to stop to help Ivanoff with his team. Fortunately, Ivanoff ran yelling after Seppala and managed to turn him back. So Seppala took the serum and headed back toward Nome.

Seppala crossed Norton Sound again. This time in blizzards and high winds, dodging melting ice and spots where the ice had moved and there was open ocean water. Shortly after they crossed, the ice collapsed and floated out to sea.

After crossing the Sound, Seppala and his team climbed a ridge to the top of Little McKinley, 5000 feet high. When Seppala reached Golovin to hand over the serum, he and his dogs had travelled 261 miles in five days.

At Golovin, Charlie Olson took the serum to Bluff and handed it over to Gunnar Kaasan.

Seppala and Kaasan were both employees of a gold-mining company. Their boss had been the one to give the dogs first to Amundsen, and when they weren't needed for an expedition, he gave them to Seppala. When the relay teams were being formed he had Kaasan use one of Seppala's dogs, Balto, as his lead dog.

Balto and Gunnar Kaasan

Balto was an almost pure-black Siberian husky. He didn't have the white markings on his face we associate with huskies, but he did have white stockings and bib. He was a large dog with a rough coat.

Leonhard Seppala had never used Balto for racing as he thought Balto was too heavy and thick. Instead, he used Balto for hauling freight. Even when hauling freight, Balto had never been used as a lead dog.

So Kaasan and Balto were 53 miles from Nome. Their job was to bring the serum to Solomon, and other teams would finish the relay to Nome. Driving through deep snow in a storm in which the snow fell so heavily that

Kaasan couldn't even see the dog closest to the sled, Balto used his nose and stayed on the main trial, missing the turn-off to Solomon. The wind was so fierce that at one point it blew the sled over and tossed the serum into the snow. Kaasan had trouble finding the serum and finally took off his gloves to search barehanded. He found the serum but suffered really bad frostbite.

When he came to Port Safety, he was 25 miles from Nome. There was another musher there who was sleeping. Instead of waiting for the other man to organize his team, Kaasan decided to keep driving to Nome. He arrive at 5:30 in the morning and collapsed. He's reported to have said "Damn fine dog" about Balto.

By late morning the serum had been thawed and given to the sick children. Nome's children were saved – all by the bravery of 20 mushers and about 150 dogs. Many of the dogs died that week and several mushers had serious frostbite injuries.

President Coolidge gave each musher a gold medal and the state gave them $25, but it was Balto and Kaasan who were treated as heroes and the other mushers and teams pretty much ignored by the public. People all over the world had followed the progression of the relay as radio telegraph news was sent out along the way. And Balto came in first.

And then ...

The newly-famous Kaasan and Balto toured the United State. Meanwhile, back in Alaska, Seppala was becoming irritated that he and his dog Togo – who had travelled the longest distance – were not recognized for what they had contributed. Plus – Balto was *his* dog. He went to his and Kaasan's boss. What was said is not known. But what happened is that Kaasan was called back to work. Not having enough money to transport the dogs home, he sold them.

Balto and his sled mates were part of a small side show for a while. After a time, the public became upset at the tacky finish of the dogs' careers which resulted in fund raising that established a home for them in the Cleveland Zoo.

Statues of Balto are in Central Park, New York City, and in Anchorage, near the start of the Iditarod Trail Sled Dog Race. (The Iditarod race began in 1973, partly to memorialize the serum run.) After their deaths, the bodies of both Balto and Togo were mounted. Balto is at a museum in Cleveland, Toga is at home – at the Iditarod museum in Wasilla.

Plan "C"

There was some very vocal opposition to using sled dogs for the vital mission. Some felt that airplanes would be a much wiser choice. Later, when a second batch of serum was being sent, they divided the shipment – half went by sled dog and half was to go by plane. The planes made several attempts but then gave up. The sled dogs delivered.

Seaman and Meriwether Lewis

Let's begin this story with the human instead of the dog.

Meriwether Lewis was born in Virginia in 1774. His father died when he was six year old and the family moved to Georgia. It was in Georgia that Lewis made friends with the local Cherokee Indians. He stayed out-of-doors most of the time. His mother taught him about the herbs used for medicine and he was curious about all the animals and plants.

Lewis was sent back to Virginia when he was 13 to be educated by tutors in his uncle's home. Later he went to college, graduated, and spend some time in the military. He left the U.S. Army as a captain in 1801 and was hired as a private secretary to Thomas Jefferson, living in the president's mansion. The Lewis family was known to Jefferson as their farm was near Jefferson's home in Virginia.

As early as 1792 – way before he became president in 1801 – Jefferson had been thinking of an expedition to the Pacific Coast. At first his interest was to find a way to go across the continent by boat – that is, to find a

Northwest Passage. He wanted an easy route all the way to the Pacific to improve trade with Asia.

Later, after he purchased the Louisiana Territory from France in 1803, Jefferson had the added need to spread the word throughout the territory that it belonged to the United States. He also wanted to spur commerce in the middle of the country in furs and other natural products to flow to the U.S. and not to other countries.

Now, back then the United States ended at the Mississippi River. The Louisiana Territory was a big chunk west of that. Then there were two pieces along the Pacific Coast: the larger southern chunk was the Spanish territory and a smaller northern piece called the Oregon Country. It was already known that you could go from the Mississippi to the Missouri River. The Missouri is the longest river in North America; while parts of it had been explored by then, many thought that the Missouri was the Northwest Passage and flow all the way to the Pacific Ocean.

Jefferson officially appointed Lewis to lead the expedition – a commissioned detail of the U.S. Army called "The Corps of Discovery" – in 1803, but he had invited Lewis years earlier to command the trip. Lewis turned to William Clark to be his co-leader. Clark had once been his superior officer in the army so making him an equal decision-maker was a smart move on Lewis' part. Lewis was 30 years old and Clark, 33.

Before the expedition began, both men were busy gathering geographical information of the regions they would pass through. Lewis had studied medicine and biology and they both studied astronomy and map making. They also found out as much as they could about the people they were likely to meet along the way.

Portrait of Meriwether Lewis

They started with a large keelboat and two pirogues, one red and one white, and a few canoes. The keelboat, designed by Lewis, was 55 foot long, 8 foot wide at the middle; it had a sail and 22 oars. The mast of this boat broke at least four times during the trip. The pirogues were smaller rowboats with sail and 6 or 7 oars.

They added men as they progressed; 59 people made part of the expedition with 30-40 men the size of the Corps on any one day. Sometimes there were also guides and their families following the Corps. One man died during the expedition – Charles Floyd from appendicitis; one child was born – to Sacajawea, the famous Indian woman who accompanied them.

The trips on the Mississippi and Missouri were upriver. Not only did they battle against the current and tricky winds, but floating logs, low water, sandbars, rapids, and waterfalls often required miles and miles of portage. Men or horses pulled the boats much of the time. Boats overturned, supplies were lost. And finally, the Missouri didn't end in the Pacific; it ended in a trickle in the Montana Mountains. They had to descend the Rockies via the Columbia River to the Pacific.

They knew of the Rockies but didn't know how high they were. They had expected peaks in the 5000-foot range.

They were lucky to cross over the Bitterroot Mountains which are low for the Rockies – about 10,000 feet; and they found a low, 5300 foot pass through them in the snow – led by a local Indian who was not sure of the way.

Lewis started alone with the keelboat from Pittsburgh on the last day of August in 1803 and reached the Pacific Ocean in November, 1805. The group wintered twice during the westward trip and again when they reached the Pacific. Lewis was a moody man and didn't keep a journal regularly; this problem persisted in his delay to write up his notes for publication. Clark also kept a journal and his spelling has amused scholars for years. They made maps that were fairly accurate. The expedition returned to St. Louis in September of 1806. The expedition sent back 120 specimens of birds, fish, reptiles and mammal as well as over 200 plants.

Lewis had many adventures and close calls: he almost died falling from a cliff, saving himself by stabbing the cliff with his lance to anchor him; he was accidentally shot by a team member; and he ran into a river and was saved from a charging grizzly bear. He did much of what Jefferson wanted, holding formal meetings with two dozen Indian tribes and meeting with trappers and others. But he did not find the Northwest Passage. The expedition was also not the first to cross the North American continent overland: Alexander Mackenzie did it crossing in Canada years before in 1793.

Their return trip from the coast was much faster – being down river and over familiar ground, and people crowded the riversides along their way when they reach populated areas. They arrived in St. Louis on September 13, 1806. The official expedition took two years, four months, and ten days and covered 8000 miles. This did not included the 2 ½ month, 1800 mile trip down the Ohio River that Lewis made with the keelboat from Pittsburgh to Louisville to meet Clark.

Many credit their expedition for sparking the migration west. On returning home, Lewis was appointed governor of the Louisiana Territory by Jefferson. He was appointed in March 1807, but didn't arrive to take up the post until March 1808. Tension between Lewis and the territory secretary, Frederick Bates, peaked when Bates publicly accused Lewis of financial mismanagement.

In 1809, Lewis left the territory to visit Washington to clear up the issue about Bates and to deliver his notes on the expedition to his publisher. Along the way, he was found dead one morning at Grinder's Stand, an inn in Tennessee. He was shot in the head and abdomen in an apparent suicide. During the trip east he'd made a will and told his companions what to do with his personal affects: that along with Lewis' known mood swings supported suicide as the cause of death. But many still believe he was murdered. He was buried near the inn. His grave was abandoned for quite some time but is now a national monument.

His notes and those of Clark were finally assembled by Nicolas Biddle and Paul Allen and published in 2014. Much later another editor, Elliott Coues, went through the notes of Lewis, Clark and others and made a more extensive report of the expedition which was published in 1893.

Seaman

Now Meriwether Lewis's dog, Seaman, is both a famous dog and a dog that not much is known about. It was years before his name was definitively recorded. And no one is *absolutely* sure he made it back all the way to St. Louis in from the Lewis & Clack expedition or what happened to him after that. Part of the mystery is caused by Lewis' off-and-on-again journal writing and his awful handwriting combined with Clark's artful spelling. Also Lewis and Clark were concentrating on longitudes and latitudes to make their maps, dealing with Indians, gathering biological specimens, and managing their men. Their journals were work products into which there were occasional notes about Seaman.

While it is known that Seaman was a large Newfoundland dog. It is not known that he was black, but everyone later assumed that he was. Lewis bought the dog for $20 when he was waiting in Pittsburgh for the keelboat to be ready. That was a lot of money back then: Lewis' monthly pay during the expedition was $40 a month. (Most farmers' income for a year was around $60). Newfoundlands are big, brave, intelligent, easy-going dogs and famous for being boat and water dogs ... retrieving game and so forth – all good reasons for Lewis getting the dog, but he never let us know exactly why he did.

A pair of typical Newfoundland dogs

So Seaman was the second member of the expedition – after Lewis. Lewis enjoyed Seaman's talent in catching squirrel on their trip down the Ohio to pick up Clark, mentioning that he'd caught many fat ones and that they'd made good eating. Seaman caught the squirrels in the river then drowned and killed them. This is the way he hunted throughout the expedition.

When they got to the meeting of the Ohio and Mississippi rivers in November of 1803, an Indian offered Lewis three beaver skins for the dog and Lewis noted that "of course there was no bargain."

Seaman isn't mentioned again until July 5, 1804. Clark wrote in his journal: "We came to for Dinner at a Beaver house. Capt. Lewis's Dog Seaman went in & drove them out."

August 1804: on a six-mile hike to see an Indian spiritual site, the dog became overheated and was sent home.

Seaman was mentioned twice by Lewis in April 1805. In the first account, Lewis had a young buffalo follow him until frightened by the sight of Seaman. Later that month, they set out early by boat. Often Seaman roamed at night but he hadn't returned yet. Lewis wrote in his journal (with his spelling): "I was fearful we had lost him altogether, however, much to my satisfaction he joined us at 8 O'clock this morning." People have interpreted this to indicate how much Lewis was attached to his dog. Lewis was a solitary creature and often walked off by himself with Seaman for company and protection.

Sgt. John Ordway also mentioned Seaman in his log in April: "Saw a flock of goats [pronghorn antelopes] swimming the river this morning near to our camp. Capt. Lewis's dog Seaman took after them, caught one in the river, drowned & killed it and swam to shore with it." Ordway was the most diligent of the journal writers, not missing a single day's entry during the expedition.

In May 1805, Seaman went into the water to fetch a beaver one of the Corps had wounded. The beaver bit the dog's hind leg and severed an artery. This time Lewis entered, "I fear it will yet prove fatal to him."

Fortunately, Seaman survived the bite and just a few days later prevented a raging buffalo bull from stomping on the heads of sleeping crew. The buffalo had stumbled over one of the pirogues when trying to come ashore. Spooked, he ran directly through their camp that night. Seaman protected the men by making the bull change his course.

Twice in June 1805 Lewis mentioned Seaman's watchdog activities. Once he prevented another bull buffalo from crossing the river to their camp. Another time he barked all night – unsuccessfully attempting to keep grizzly bears from getting the buffalo fat they had hanging from a pole quite a distance from camp. The grizzlies managed to eat thirty pounds or so of the fat.

The following month, Lewis twice praised Seaman's water hunting skills. The first time, one of the party had wounded a deer and it ran into the river. Seaman chased it, drowned and killed it. A few weeks later, Seaman captured and killed several geese.

Prickly pear cactus was the bane of the trip. Blankets of the cactus lined much of their route along the Missouri river. The barbs penetrated their moccasins and leggings causing additional damage to feet bruised and battered from walking on rocks. When they stopped for winter on the Pacific coast, they made 338 new pairs of moccasins with double soles but these still let the barbs pierce the skin. Foxtail, a grass, has seeds that were also a constant irritant. In July 1806, Lewis wrote how they also affected Seaman: "my poor dog suffers with them excessively, he is constantly biting and scratching himself in a rack of pain."

Sacagawea had been stolen from an area near where the Missouri meets the Rockies. When they neared the places she'd known as a child she recognized some of the landmarks and helped the Corps reach her brother. They had hoped he could provide horses for their trek over the mountains. When they finally reached her tribe, Lewis remarked of their impressions of the Corps and of Seaman: "Every article about us appeared to excite astonishment in their minds; the appearance of the men, their arms, the canoes, our manner of working them, the black man York and the sagacity of my dog were equally objects of admiration."

There was no mention of Seaman in the journals from August 1805 to April 11, 1806. In crossing the Rockies both food and firewood were scarce and the Indians less friendly. Some thefts occurred as well. In addition, forty of their horses were stolen during their trip home. On April 11, three Wallala Chinook men stole Seaman and fled. Chased by armed men of the Corps they released the dog. After that, Lewis posted additional guards whenever they camped.

On July 5, 1806, Lewis had seen swans on a pretty creek and admired them. Leaving, he made a note in his journal that he'd call the creek "Seaman's Creek". Years later, in 1987, a researcher came across the note and realized Seaman must've been Lewis's dog's name. Up until then everyone thought the dog's name was Scannon – and many other dogs wore that name in honor of the expedition.

On July 7, 1806, Lewis wrote that someone had wounded a moose and "my dog was much worried."

The next and last mention Seaman in Lewis's journals was on July 15, 1806. Mosquitoes had been thick and torturing the Corps. "[T]he mosquitoes continue to infest us in such manner that we can scarcely exist; for my own part I am confined by them to my bier at least 3/4 the of the time. My dog even howls with the torture he experiences from them".

What happened to Seaman?

There is not further mention of Seaman in any of the expedition journals. It is thought that Seaman returned from the trip based upon two things: if Seaman had died, he was important enough so that someone would have recorded his death in one of their journals. While Lewis wasn't the most regular of scribes, all the sergeants were required to make a daily record and Clark barely missed a day in writing in his.

The other reason for thinking Seaman returned was found by Timothy Alden, a preacher and historian. He published a book in 1814, *American Epitaphs and Inscriptions*. Entry 916 contained information about a dog's collar in a Virginia museum. The entry included both what was inscribed on the collar and what was in the note that accompanied it. Later a thank you note was found from the museum to William Clark for the "curiosities" he'd given the museum. A museum fire has prevented any further research on this, but many think it's reasonable that Clark had given Seaman's collar to the museum and written the note."

The dog's collar was inscribed: "The greatest traveler of my species. The name is SEAMAN, the dog of captain Meriwether Lewis whom I accompanied to the Pacific Ocean through the interior of the continent of North America."

The contents of the note: "The fidelity and attachment of this animal were remarkable. After the melancholy exit of gov. Lewis, his dog would not depart for a moment from his lifeless remains; and when they were deposited in the earth no gentle means could draw him from the spot of interment. He refused to take every kind of food, which was offered him, and actually pined away and died with grief upon his master's grave."

As the story of Seaman's death was reported in newspapers and many of the expedition members were alive to refute it, it is believed the story to be true.

Almo and Christensen

At the end of World War I, there were 2800 German soldiers who survived but who were left blinded from mustard gas. Another soldier, Lambert Kreimer, had been badly wounded in the war. Lying in the hospital, Kreimer was moved by these young blind men. They had to wait for everything – someone to get things for them, someone to take them for walks, someone to drive them somewhere. These men spent hours waiting. Kreimer thought of them as prisoners of war, really.

Kreimer was a dog breeder and had trained police dogs before the war. And he'd also trained them to do all kinds of tricks for him. When he returned to civilian life and his German shepherd dogs, he started to figure out a way for them to help the blind veterans. He devised a training program for one dog, Rolf, and worked with one blind veteran.

When they was ready, he went back to the hospital. The blind veterans and their "seeing-eye persons" gathered outside and watched as Rolf and his blind veteran were able to walk by themselves down the sidewalks, across streets, up and down stairs, in and out of the hospital, while avoiding things put in the way to trip them up – all with no problem at all. When the blind men heard what how well Rolf and the veteran were doing, they broke out cheering wildly.

The government became interested and started the first school to train dogs and blind veterans in Munich. Kreimer was in charge of training. It took three to six months to train each dog, but the veterans learned to use the dogs in just a few weeks. Germany established three others schools and within ten years more than 2,000 veterans had dogs – through these schools and others that had been established later.

It wasn't an entirely new idea to use dogs to guide the blind. Ancient wall paintings showed dogs leading the blind. But earlier techniques involved having the dog on a leash with the blind person following with or without a cane.

The dog harness had been tried once, a hundred years before, by a doctor in Vienna. A stick attached to the dog's collar had a crossbar that gave the blind a more direct feeling of the dog's movements side to side. But this idea wasn't tried again for a hundred years.

The harness idea was resurrected during this time after the war and was very similar to the leather harness seen today. A harness gives the blind a more delicate feeling of the dogs' movements and also slows the dog's pace down and lets it know that it's "working dog time".

Almo

Almo was born in the Black Forest region of Germany. His owner was a gardener as well as a breeder of German shepherds and trainer of police dogs. Almo was born with six sisters and brothers. The smartest dog of the litter, Almo became the owner's favorite. They roamed the forest and played, but also began training to be a police dog. This meant that Almo was trained not to try to make friends with anyone other than his handler. He could deliver messages and return without stopping, ignoring any other dogs along the way. He ran ahead of his handler, ready to attack anyone threatening them. He learned to track people by their scent – in both the city and out in the country.

When Almo was 18 months old, his owner sold him to a police department for a lot of money. Both the owner and Almo were sad to separate, but the owner needed extra money for Christmas to provide for his family. In the police station, Almo lay on the floor that first night whining.

Sometime later, Almo was recognized as extremely talented and assigned to be trained as a guide dog. After he was trained, Almo and four other dogs were taken by our old friend Lambert Kreimer to the United States. Kreimer was coming to take a new job as a trainer in Minneapolis/St. Paul.

At that time, guide dogs were rarely seen in the U.S.

Typical German Sheppard

William A. Christensen

Until he was 16, William Christensen lived in South Florida. His father ran a fleet of sponge boats and William lived a life among horses, dogs, cats, and adventures at sea. He learned to roll cigars and attended university. He had hoped to become an architect but his father died and his plans changed. He started a cigar company with a friend. Later they switched to distributing food products.

Well on his way to becoming a successful business owner, there was a smallpox epidemic. Christensen was 29 when he got vaccinated to prevent the disease. For some reason, the vaccine attacked his body. His muscles wasted, he became blind and was expected to die. Slowly his body recovered -- except for his eyes. He was not just blind but experienced terrible eye pain for the next 16 years until surgery to the nerves stopped the pain.

Sick, in pain, Christensen slowly searched for how to earn his living. His recovery was helped by meeting and then marrying his wife. He finally started a business distributing paper products. To do this, he memorized the product lists and prices of the various manufacturers and slowly acquired clients. Later his business grew to distribute a wide variety of merchandise.

The Meeting

A Mr. Sinykin in St. Paul/Minneapolis raised German shepherds as a hobby. He'd heard of the guide dog effort in Germany and, after some time, managed to buy two trained dogs. These he'd sold and was amazed by how much these dogs could help their blind owners. He decided to start training his own dogs to guide the blind. At first he had trouble finding trainers but finally he hired Lambert Kreimer from Germany to come.

Sinykin travelled around the country telling how wonderful guide dogs were. William Christensen happened to meet Sinykin in Hollywood and listened to his tales for hours. Later when he heard Sinykin had hired Kreimer and that Kreimer was coming with dogs already trained, he asked to buy one. It was arranged that Kreimer would come with two dogs for Christensen to choose from.

When Christensen finally met the dogs, he ran his hands all over the first one and talked to it. When the meeting finished, the dog went and sat at the trainer's feet and was then taken away. When the second dog came in,

Christensen could feel it was larger. And this dog was quieter, less nervous as he handled him. When William was through, the second dog lay at his feet instead of by the trainer. And he extended his neck and licked Christensen's hand. This silenced the people in the room who knew that trained guide dogs were supposed to attend to their handler. The second dog, of course, was Almo.

Christensen had to learn the German words Almo knew as he and Almo were being trained to work together. Later, though, Almo learned English. Christensen had been blind for 14 years and had never used a cane, so he needed to learn how to use it to measure curb and step heights. Watched by the trainer, Christensen learned to walk straight and not walk all over Almo's feet. By the second week, he and Almo were crossing busy streets by themselves. Almo needed Christensen to know exactly where he was going. He learned to count streets and give the right commands.

Later, when Almo was familiar with the neighborhood, he needed just a single command to bring Christensen directly to places they visited often, such as the pharmacy and – Almo's favorite – the butcher shop. Early in the morning and late at night they enjoyed taking long walks.

Christensen's life became even better when, two years after Almo came, he had the surgery on his eyes to stop the pain. After that, Christensen and Almo travelled all over the United States.

Hero Dog

Christensen and Almo had travelled more than 100,000 miles together when they and Christensen's wife were guests at an inn in Oakland, California. Knowing Christensen liked peace and quiet, the owner put them by themselves on the third (and top) floor. Tired from travel, they were napping when Almo whined and nudged Christensen until he woke up.

This was unusual for Almo to do, so Christensen put the harness on Almo and went to investigate. He could hear a commotion on the floors below but his floor was quiet. He decided things were okay and commanded Almo to go back to the room. But Almo refused, even jumping up on Christensen. Then sounds began, glass crashing, crackling of fire.

Christensen went back and got his wife. Smoke was so thick by then she could barely see. Almo put his nose close to the ground, trying to find fresh air. Weaving among the corridors, Almo brought them to a tiny window leading to a narrow ladder to a roof below. When they opened the window, the draft made the fire more fierce and move closer to them. A fireman came to the top of the ladder to help.

Christensen and his wife tried again and again to squeeze Almo through the tiny window to the waiting fireman. Finally, Christensen realized the dog wouldn't leave the building while Christensen was still inside. So he left, and after many attempts, he and his wife talked the fireman through how to lift the dog out of the window. The fireman had wanted them to abandon Almo, but they had refused.

Safe, Almo led them across a series of roofs to the ground and calmly took them to their car. Sitting in the quiet car together, muting the hubbub surrounding the fire. Shortly, though, reporters surrounded them wanting to know every detail of Almo's feat.

It turned out the fire was started by an electrical short on the top floor and had burned behind the walls and above the ceilings until it burst out.

National press made Almo a hero. For the rest of his life he received many awards and medals for bravery as well as his guiding talents. When he died, Christensen had him preserved by a taxidermist, complete with his harness.

Lasse and Amundsen

Lasse and Roald Amundsen were among the first to first reach the South Pole. Before telling their story, just a few words about the poles:

The Poles

Ancient astronomers had figured out that the earth was round and that it turned on its axis from west to east each day. They had even calculated the size of the earth within 0.5%. Over the following centuries, scientists and explorers filled in the details of the globe with longitude and latitude refinements and the technology to determine them.

The north and south poles are simply where the earth's axis ends at its surface, and are directly opposite each other. Explorers wanted to be first in finding the poles were.

The North Pole is over the open sea and is covered with big ice blocks. The sea is more than 13,000 feet deep at that point. In 1908 Frederick Cook claimed he stood at the North Pole but reviews of his records by a commission ruled he had insufficient proof.

Robert Peary then claimed he had reached the North Pole in 1909. His claim was accepted for years, but now it is thought he may just have come within sixty miles of the pole but did not reach it.

Roald Amundsen flew over the North Pole in 1926. Curiously, the first person to reach the North Pole on foot wasn't until a Russian expedition did it in1948. The Russians had flown in and landed near the pole. The North Pole is now a regular tourist attraction.

The South Pole is over land, in the continent of Antarctica. Reports of the continent being sighted were made in the early 1800s. Robert Scott explored the continent in 1902 with Ernest Shackleton; they reached 80°S. (90°S is the South Pole.) Shackleton came back in 1909 and reached 88°S.

Lasse

Lasse grew up in North Greenland, a division of Greenland on the northwest coast. This was sled dog country. The dogs are bred to work. The dogs, once called Eskimo dogs, are now called Greenland dogs. Lasse was almost pure black, but the dogs come in all colors and have a thick woolly undercoat and a waterproof overcoat that keeps them warm at very low temperatures. The dogs are an ancient breed in the Spitz group of dogs and have that group's curled tail and short triangular ears.

When Amundsen ordered 100 dogs, Lasse was in the group. They were shipped to Norway on a steam merchant ship, the Hans Egeda. (The ship was sunk by a German U-boat in 1942.) The dogs had a long hard sail over and made it to Norway in bad condition. They were kept in an ancient fortress for over a month before boarding Anderson's boat, Fram. The deck for the dogs had been constructed using a raised floor so air could circulate on warm days, and if water came onto the deck the dogs were above it.

Lasse's given name was Lars, but Lasse and Lassesen were his nicknames. In his book of the expedition, Amundsen wrote of how Lasse was the wildest dog to come on board the boat and that it took weeks to tame him – at first Lasse bared his teeth whenever he walked near him. Amundsen tried patting him with a stick and the dog broke it in two. They kept Lasse tied near Fix, his friend from Greenland, in hopes he'd simmer down.

Roald Amundsen

Amundsen was a Norwegian. His family was one of ship owners and ship captains. His mother wanted a different life for him, so he began studying medicine. His mother died when he was 21 and he promptly left college and went to sea. He'd been tempted by the stories of the explorers of the period and decided that was a life he wanted for himself.

On Amundsen's first ship, on a Belgian exploration of the waters around Antarctica, he was a first mate. Amundsen got his first taste of adventure when the ship got iced in and spent the winter there, the first ship to ever do that. He also learned how to avoid scurvy on that trip: Frederick Cook was the ship's doctor and supplied the ship with fresh meat to give them a supply of Vitamin C.

Amundsen soon led his own expeditions. Explorers had long tried to navigate the waters north of Canada to find the Northwest Passage – a one-way trip from the Atlantic to the Pacific Ocean. Amundsen bought a small boat that floated high in the water, and with a crew of 5 others made the complete voyage from 1903 to 1906 by following closely to shore. Twice they wintered on King Williams Island. It was during these winters that he learned about sled dogs and wearing animal skins for warmth. He had always known how to ski but learned that skiing along with dog sleds was the fastest method over land.

Amundsen's Plan for the North Atlantic – and Change of Plans

Amundsen's next adventure was to leave in the summer of 2010 to probe the ice fields in the north Atlantic and to be first to reach the North Pole. His boat, the Fram, had been used in arctic waters on other expeditions. It was a short fat boat with a rounded bottom. The design allowed the boat to simply rise above freezing ice rather than be crushed by it.

He selected his crew and meticulously outfitted it for the trip north. However, in September 2009 newspapers reported that both Scott and Peary had reached the North Pole. While Amundsen's north Atlantic trip had some scientific goals, he really wanted to be the first to the North Pole. So, in secret, Amundsen decided to compete to be the first to reach the South Pole. He told only his brother and the man who would captain his ship.

He quickly ordered 100 dogs from Greenland as well the sleds, harnesses, and food for the dogs. The ship's last stop in Norway was in Kristiansand. The crew was confused to see all the dogs and the equipment being loaded, as the arctic trip was planning stops in Alaska where there were plenty of dogs and sleds. It wasn't until they reached Madeira, a group of Islands west of Morocco owned by Portugal, that he told the crew of his plans and gave them an opportunity to leave. None did.

In Madeira, he also sent a telegram to Robert Scott who was already on his way to attempt to reach the South Pole on his second try. Later, Amundsen received a lot of bad press in England for "sneaking" down to the south.

The Fram was a three-masted sailing ship with a Swedish engine. It even had a windmill to power electric lights. The boat was well stocked. There were sections for a sturdy hut he had built; it would be 26 by 13 feet and included a 6 by 13 foot kitchen. In addition to 97 dogs, there were 19 men, four pigs, six carrier pigeons, and a canary. There were skis, lumber, cloth, clothing, tents, and navigation equipment. Over 3000 books were loaded. Amundsen had carefully calculated the food they would need and added enough spirits to allow a small sip on Saturday and Sunday nights. They even had a record player and a few records.

They reached Antarctica on December 14, 2010. Amundsen anchored Fram in the Bay of Whales. He knew that Scott would be at McMurdo Sound, and follow the same direction that Shackleton had. Scott and would have 60 more miles to go to the pole, but Amundsen would have find his own way over the mountains while Scot would follow Shackleton's route.

When they anchored, the men made a camp two miles inland. First, they dug a four foot foundation for the hut, then assembled it. It wasn't until January 27 that the hut was finished and all the material had been moved to the inland site. Tents and snow caves were used to store material and the dogs. This time allowed the men to arrange the dogs in working teams and train them.

Next they made three trips to store material to be used along their route to the pole. These trips took from February 10 to April 11 during which they stored 7500 pounds of food and supplies. On these trips they found that six dogs per sled were not enough and decided they would take more dogs and fewer men on the trip to the pole.

The sun set on April 21 and they would have four months without it. Amundsen set a regular schedule of work for the men. During this time they reconstructed the sleds, making them 30% lighter. They made skis and lightweight tents with floors. They made biscuits and pemmican for the trip.

Amundsen and men in the hut in Antarctica. Amundsen is 5th from left.

Setting off!

Anxious to begin, they set out for the South Pole on September 8. At one point the temperature dipped to -69°. The dogs' feet froze and two dogs froze to death while sleeping. It was too cold for the men to sleep. On the third day they returned to the hut to wait for warmer weather.

On October 19 they set out again with 52 dogs, four sleds, and five men. They were pleased at the speed the dogs made on the smooth surface. Each day at lunch they build a cairn ... a mound a few feet high, with notes inside of the direction to the last cairn and the direction they were heading. These cairns made the return trip go smoothly.

To those of us not sled dog explorers, expeditions like this seem cruel. Amundsen admired the sled dogs, but they were work dogs, not pets. The sad fact of their lives was that on long trips most were expected to die. The way other men ran dogs was to run them until they died from exhaustion, then feed their meat to the surviving dogs. Amundsen planned use more dogs than others would. He planned to kill most of them humanely, not work them to death. They were saddened by the deaths of the dogs, but it was a fact of life for them that the meat was needed for survival of the dogs who would finish the expedition.

On November 21, there were 42 dogs alive when they reached the 10,000 foot summit of the Transantarctic

Mountains, the longest mountain range in the world. There, as planned, they shot 24 of the dogs. Each man butchered his own dogs. It was a somber evening when the task was complete. The surviving dogs were allowed to eat as much of the meat as they wanted. The dog meat was also made into a soup for the men. The remaining meat was buried in snow for the trip back. They stayed for several days on the summit waiting for the weather to clear. The finally left what they called The Butcher's Shop, descended the mountain then began the more gradual climb to the South Pole.

On December 8 they passed Shackleton's mark of 88°S, 95 miles from the pole. When they neared the South Pole on December 14, they urged Amundsen to walk ahead so he would be the first man to reach it. They stayed at the pole for three days to calculate the most precise location of the pole. Then they erected a tent and left a note for Scott.

Oscar Wisting at the South Pole on December 14, 1911
Lasse was running on Wisting's team when they reached the South Pole. He's thought to be the dark dog at the front.

With lighter sleds and knowing the way back, they returned to the hut on January 25, 1912, with 2 sleds and 11 dogs. It had taken 99 days to travel 1860 miles.

The men loaded the Fram with equipment and supplies quickly and left Antarctica on January 30. They reached

Tasmania on March 7, where Amundsen could telegraph their success to his brother.

What happened to Scott?

Scott left his base camp four days after Amundsen. He reached the South Pole January 18, 2012, 35 days behind Amundsen.

Scott reached the South Pole but died with four others on the way back. Much has been written of his mistakes. He relied on motorized sleds and ponies, having just a few dogs. The motorized sleds failed and the ponies died or had to be killed. Scott had to use men to pull the sleds much of the way. He'd also undersupplied the expedition – with many more men, he had a third of the supplies as Amundsen had. He used all wool clothes while Amundsen had animal skins and fur for the colder times. Amundsen also had lightweight material for times the men might sweat while skiing. Finally, Scott had supplies enough for four men for the final push to the Pole but took five men instead. He also had fewer supply depots pre-placed before beginning.

Lasse and Amundsen endings

Sadly, Lasse made it to the South Pole but was the first dog killed on the way back, on December 19. Amundsen wrote that he was he favorite dog but had worn himself out completely.

Amundsen died in 1928 in a plane crash in the arctic. He was with a group looking to rescue a lost dirigible. He was 55 years old.

Bothy with Ranulph & Virginia Fiennes

It was a crazy idea. Many people had gone around the world the horizontal way, but Virginia Fiennes had this idea of going vertically while staying on the surface of the earth.

Her husband, Ranulph ... or Ran from here on ... said it would be impossible ... they'd have to travel so that they went across each pole, north and south. It had never been done and it would be insane to try. Ran was a 'sir' – a British baronet – but he had no money. They lived on his lectures and writing from a few treks he'd taken already. He and Ginnie, as she was called, had been married just over a year.

Ran had been on a few adventures. He'd crossed British Columbia by river and climbed a Norwegian Glacier. They'd gone up the Nile by Hovercraft together. Ginnie organized all their trips.

They returned to the "bipolar" idea again and again. The more negative feedback they got, the more they wanted to try it. They played with a tiny six-inch globe to see what route they could take. They were pretty sure the Russians wouldn't let them in areas they controlled, so decided the route should follow the Greenwich meridian – the imaginary line running north/south through Greenwich, England. They also thought that this route, beginning and ending in England, would help them get the English support they'd need. They'd need a lot of money, government support, plus support of the exploring community.

It took from early 1972 to September 1979 for the expedition to begin. On board the ship leaving from the Greenwich Pier were HRH Prince Charles, Ran, Ginnie, the ice team and the boat team. Bothy, their long-haired terrier mix, stayed home – Africa would've been too hot for him.

What took them so long to get started?

The hurdles were enormous. They had no money. They had no polar experience. They had no scientific reason for going. Every government and scientific group said "no".

They whittled away at the problems.

Ran still gave weekends to the Special Air Services (SAS) of the British Army. The SAS provided a windowless attic room with no phone for them to begin planning. They stole phones and later got promoted to the first floor. Some of their volunteers slept in the office. Finally they were able to get donated office space on Baker Street with three phones.

With the short windows to travel across each pole, they figured it would take at least three years to complete the trip. On each pole they needed light, not too cold weather, but not so warm that the snow and ice would melt. Somehow they managed to find crew for a boat, office staff, expedition support staff, and most of the pilots of the planes – who were willing to set aside their jobs and work for no pay. They were able to connect with hundreds of companies to give the equipment and supplies – including fuel, loan of pilots, planes, and ship captains. In addition, donations of cash helped in emergencies and to buy their ship.

They were advised to go by snowmobile as it would add two years to the preparation for the men to be trained to work with dogs. They were also concerned about possible bad publicity – normally on long dog treks, dogs either die or are killed and used as food for dogs and men.

Prince Charles agreed to be Patron of the expedition. He was key in getting some of the governments to cooperate and finding people willing to contribute.

They worked with scientists and were able to add Antarctic ice research, medical research, and Army equipment/food/clothing research to their mission. They even collected specimens in Africa for British Natural History Museum.

They trained with the SAS. In 1976 they made a practice run in Greenland. And finally, they made an attempt to reach the North Pole in early 1979. The North Pole attempt was aborted in May as the sea ice had turned to slush and they needed to be rescued.

Much of their route was over water. They were going from England to Europe by ferry and drive through France and Spain. Then, a short boat trip to Africa where they'd drive through the "bulge" of western Africa, going from Algeria and Mali to the Ivory Coast. Next they'd take their ship to South Africa and on to Antarctica where they'd land at Sanae (South African National Expedition). They would base an airstrip at Sanae for a plane to supply their route across the continent to McMurdo Sound. They'd winter at a base camp about 300 miles inland, at the foothills of the Borga Mountains. Their trek would be the first across the continent going north/south and the longest trip across Antarctica.

After Antarctica, they'd go by ship to Alaska. They'd go by small motor boat up the Yukon River to the north of the country, then go east, making an attempt to pass over the sea ice to the North Pole. They'd complete the Northwest Passage by meeting their boat in the Atlantic and go home to Greenwich. They would be just the second group to traverse the Arctic Ocean and the first to combine it with reaching the Atlantic Ocean.

Ran

Ran made the entire trip. Oliver Shepard and Charles Burton were with Ran crossing Antarctica and Burton man made the whole trip. Shepard left after Antarctica to be with his wife. When Ran wanted to do the arctic trip with just two men their advisory board of polar experts back in London attempted to cancel the expedition.

Ginnie

Ginnie was with the expedition boat trips and drove one of the Land Rovers from France to the Ivory Coast with her vehicle crammed with radio equipment. She flew to be with Ran at both poles. Other times she was stationed close enough to Ran to operate radios to stay in contact with him. Often she *was* the base camp in addition to her radio work. She drove with Bothy to meet Ran during the Northwest Passage trip. From the beginning, Ginnie was the organizer. She was able to supply Ran's need for different snowmobiles and boats. She arranged planes to scout the sea ice and deliver supplies. Sometimes she could make contact using only Morse code and sat by the radio for hours to find a connection and tap out messages.

Bothy

Bothy had been found wandering the streets as a four-month-old pup and given to the Fiennes. The name "Bothy" is Brit/Scot slang for an outhouse. (Note: In his book of the trip, Ran spelled the dog's name "Bothy". Later it was spelled "Bothie" in their book, *Bothie the Polar Dog*.) The Fiennes said he was a mongrel but he's often called a Jack Russell Terrier in articles. He was white with a few brown patches.

Ship to Antarctica. Bothy joined the ship at Cape Town, South Africa. Bothy had a character flaw – he was house-trained but not ship-trained. On board ship he made himself a constant nuisance and safety hazard with his "gifts" on the decks. People were slipping and sliding whenever they walked into the dark places that he chose. He also placed his gifts in any stateroom with a door left open. Finally he discovered a green rubber mat the crew had used for sunbathing and declared it his own private lawn.

Bothy didn't need to find someone to play ball with him onboard ship – the ship's tossing in the sea bounced his rubber balls all over the place for him to chase. The trip was rough, the waves were high, and Bothy was thrown around several times, but survived the three-week, 2400-mile trip (as the crow flies). He wore a safety harness much of the time when on deck.

Antarctica. Bothy's job on the expedition was to be with Ginnie at all the base camps. He and Ginnie were flown to the Borga base camp and helped assemble the cardboard buildings and radio antennas. The three men on the ice team traveled there by snowmobile from the ship's landing site. From early January to October 28, they lived in the cardboard buildings. At night the temperature on the floor dropped to 5°F; they slept on platforms near the ceiling where the temperature was a balmy 28°F.

Ran built ice tunnels connecting the buildings so they minimized the time they were exposed to the cold air. Ginnie was claustrophobic so there were no tunnels to the radio hut. There were too many exposed wires in the radio hut so at first Bothy stayed most of the time in the main hut with Burton who was expedition cook. Burton complained in his diary about Ginnie taking Bothy on the expedition, but leaving him alone all day for him to take care of. However, Burton seemed amused as he played catch with Bothy several hours a day. Later, Ginnie kept Bothy in a shed during the day.

They had to be careful not to let Bothy go outside. Wind chill could be as severe as minus 110°F and kill the little dog in minutes. When Bothy did venture out he was bundled in a red polar suit, boots, and a head cover that left just his eyes and mouth exposed.

In the buildings, Bothy continued to refuse guidance in where he deposited his gifts – presenting one in Burton's boot once. Ran's job was cleaning so he hunted for Bothy's deposits every day.

They had been together from early January to October 1981 when the three men left to climb the mountain in front of them and continue crossing Antarctica. It was minus 58°F the morning they left. Simon, who'd been down at Sanae, moved in with Ginnie and Bothy to run the generators. When the men reached McMurdo Station on the other side of the continent, Ginnie and Bothy flew to be there when they arrived.

Bothy had to be kept outside in a separate tent to avoid his contact with the sled dogs there to avoid passing any "outside" viruses to them. (In 1993 dogs were permanently banned from Antarctica as canine distemper was infecting the seals.)

After waiting for their ship to arrive (it took on charter business when not needed for the expedition to add some revenue), the team was off again. This time up the Pacific Ocean to Alaska's Yukon River. They stopped in Sydney Australia for Bothy to meet Prince Charles. One hot day they stopped the ship and they all, including Bothy, had a swim.

Arctic. They reached the Yukon River June 30, 1981. In the arctic, Ginnie had to move her base camps to keep in touch by radio with Ran. Sometimes they were in small settlements, sometimes in deserted cabins alone. One base camp she ran from a garage/inn; to pay for a room and telephone service she waited tables and washed dishes. At one time, the shed they used to store spare snowmobiles, equipment, and fuel caught fire and everything was lost.

The most idyllic spot was Tanquary Camp. They were alone at the end of August, 1981. With two dogs now. Ginnie had rescued Tugulak, a pup she rescued from the Inuits; they were going to kill it as there was a surplus of dogs there. It had been a tiny black thing when she first got it but she was soon quite large. Bothy loved her. At Tanquary they chased after hares, observed closely by wolves. Ran couldn't decide if the wolves thought the dogs would taste good or if they were just curious – but several adults with their pups often stayed close to the hut.

They wintered at Alert, Canada. Alert is the most northern point with year-round inhabitants. The inhabitants are temporary military and scientific staff for the radio and weather operations there. Ran and Barton left on February 13 by snowmobile. They reached the North Pole on April 10, 1982. They were on an ice floe that was getting slushy. Bothy arrived by plane and showed his interest by nearly peeing on the Union Jack they'd planted. Just a few days later a plane with tourists landed at the same spot on the floe and sank.

This was the end of Bothy's expedition. Both he and Tugulak were flown to England for a six-month quarantine. Bothy's biggest contribution was being his yappy silly self, bolstering the spirits of everyone on the expedition. They laughed at his running away fearfully from his first penguin. They admired his nonchalance

66

with the wolves and his bravery in facing the moose. He and Ginnie both believed they'd seen ghosts.

Bothy was the first and only dog to touch both poles. It cannot be repeated as dogs are now banned at the South Pole. Ran and Ginnie wrote a book, *Bothie, the Polar Dog*, of the dog's exploits with them. Bothy was named Dog of the Year by the UK Kennel Club. Ginnie bred Tugulak and apparently started a new breed with several descendants.

The scary parts for Ran

In Antarctica it was the fields of crevasses – any one of which could swallow them whole. It was tricky timing the trip ... they needed daylight and it had to warm up enough so they wouldn't freeze to death. But as the sun rose higher, the snow and ice that bridged the crevasses evaporated, increasing the danger of falling into them.

The Arctic was the most grueling and the most dangerous part of the expedition. While they had snowmobiles, they didn't just rev them up and ride off to the pole. There were huge blocks of ice, much like thick tables on end that were five to forty feet high. They had to use their axes to cut most of their way to the North Pole.

And they were over open seas riding on blocks of ice. One time Ran fell into the water, which could've easily killed him. He managed to crawl back onto the ice and Burton found him in time to erect a makeshift tent and warm him up.

The most harrowing part of the trip was after they'd reached the pole and started toward the Atlantic Ocean. Ice was breaking apart. The trick was to find a large floe and camp on it at just the right time so the currents would propel them east. They found a floe and pitched their tents. As the weather warmed there were calls from England to abort the trip before the floe broke up and they'd be lost.

One day they "lost two acres" from their floe. Then it got so slushy they had to wear hip boots to walk on the solid parts of it   Large lakes formed.   Then polar bears started visiting every day.

But – after three months on the ice floe – they made it! They reached the ship on August 4 and were back in Greenwich on August 29 after Ran's travelling about 52,000 miles over three years. Ran has gone on other adventures, losing many fingertips on one of them. Ginnie became the first woman to belong to the Antarctic

Club and received the Polar medal from the Queen. She died at 56 in 2004.

Chips and the Wrens

Chips was three weeks old when he was given to the Wards. Chips looked like a German shepherd, but was a mutt – his father a German shepherd and his mother a mix of collie and with some husky and/or shepherd. The Ward's two daughters loved the dog. Chips grew to be an active, healthy dog. There was one problem: Chips was protective of the girls ... perhaps too much so. One day he "defended" the girls again a garbage man and bit him.

U.S. military dogs

At that time, the attack on Pearl Harbor had occurred and the United States had entered World War II. Unlike many countries, the United States did not have an official dog corps in World War I. The U.S. gave several hundred dogs to the French to be used to carry ammunition in the mountains, but when the U.S. entered the First World War the military had to borrow trained dogs from its allies.

So, another war comes and the U.S. had still not made any effort to add dogs to its military despite the value the dogs had shown in previous wars all over the world. The only dogs in service when the Second World War started were a few sled dogs in Alaska. Civilians worried about the security along America's coasts and, in January 1942, formed Dogs for Defense (DFD). DFD consisted of the American Kennel Club, breeders, trainers, and finance people who offered to collect and train sentry dogs for the Coast Guard and Army at no cost to the military.

A pilot project by the DFD was begun but hampered by training done by so many different people in small numbers with no single training method. Also, the military was not involved in training, so military handlers weren't trained how to work with the dogs. So in March the Army's Quartermaster Corps took over responsibility of acquiring and training sentry dogs. In the summer of 1942, the secretary of war ordered the Corps to begin training dogs for activities in addition to sentry. The Corps' first dog reception and training center opened in Front Royal, Virginia, in August 1942.

Chips is "volunteered"

Just as Mr. Wren became concerned that Chips was too aggressive, the publicized request for donations of family dogs to the war dog effort got his attention. The family decided to donate Chips in August 1942. Chips was sent to Front Royal.

During the war 10,000 dogs were trained by the Corps, but most were trained for sentry duty. Just 571 dogs were trained as scouts and Chips was one of them. Another 300 dogs were trained for delivering messages or for sniffing mines.

It took eight to twelve weeks for the training. Scout training involved all the training given to sentry dogs – primarily to alert their handler to any strangers nearby – plus they learned to work quietly, to snoop out the enemy.

Chips was trained with his handler, John P. Rowell, a private from Arkansas. Their first assignment was to the 3rd Division Infantry.

Chip's ID in the army was Brand #11A. He was among the first group of dogs sent outside of the states.

Action Begins!

Chips landed in one of the most active divisions. The 3rd division fought for 531 days in a row. Chips was in 8 separate "theaters" or combat areas beginning in North Africa, then Sicily, Italy, France, and Germany – often with Patton's 7th Army.

Little is available about Chips activities in North Africa, except for a story about when Chips and Rowell landed on the beach in French Morocco. In November, 1942, they landed under heavy fire so Lowell made shallow holes for them each to hide in. Then Lowell started digging himself deeper into the sand for greater protection. Chips, no dummy, saw what he was doing and started digging himself a proper foxhole.

At some point in his career, Chips warned his handler of enemies nearby during active shooting. They attached a phone wire to Chips collar and he dodged his was back to their base so the platoon could call for reinforcements.

In January 1943 President Roosevelt, Prime Minister Churchill, and their military chiefs met in Constantinople (now Istanbul), Turkey. Their meeting was to plan the strategy for attacking Europe. At that time, Chips was assigned to headquarters and was one of the three sentry dogs guarding the President. He worked 12-hour shifts with his handler.

Actions above and beyond the call of duty

Chips was in the thick of it in Sicily. The invasion began during the night of July 9, 1943. Before dawn, Chips and

Rowell had moved from their landing craft to the beach. Battle noises were loud as their platoon tried to get inland. They were headed toward what they thought was an old grass-covered hut they could use for shelter when machine gun fire from the hut nailed them to the ground. They'd disturbed an Italian machine-gun nest. Chips, ignoring all his training to stay with and obey his handler, broke away from Rowell. They heard him snarling as he ran right into the hut. The soldiers then heard a lot of noise from the hut followed by a pistol shot. The machine-gun firing stopped, followed by an Italian soldier coming out of the hut with Chips' teeth locked on his throat. Chips finally obeyed Rowell and released his grip as the three other soldiers came out of the hut and surrendered. Surrendered to Chips, really.

The pistol had been fired at Chips, but the bullet lightly grazed his head. Medics treated the bullet wound and powder burns of his face, mouth & tongue, and his eye. Chips went right back on duty with Lowell. That night on guard duty Chips used his sentry skills to alert Rowell to ten enemy soldiers trying to enter the camp. Lowell and Chips captured them all.

The division commander awarded Chips a Purple Heart for his wounds and a Silver Star for his bravery in action. The actual medals came and were awarded to Chips in a churchyard ceremony in Italy on November 18, 1943. The commander also put Chips in for the Distinguished Service Cross.

Chips

Chips fame didn't stop his work assignments. He continued to campaigns in Italy – to both Salerno and Rome. In September, 1943, after success at Salerno, General Eisenhower visited the platoon to congratulate them on their success. Like most men when they meet dogs, Ike leaned over to pat Chips on the head. Chips, a well-trained sentry dog, could only be touched by his handler. He quickly bit the famous President-to-be. Around the troops, he was as famous for that as for his battle exploits.

Chips continued to go with his unit north through Europe until the War's end.

Leaving

The war came to an end in Europe in May, 1945; this ended the campaigns that Chips fought in. When Japan surrendered in September, 1945, World War II was finally over. Chips was returned to the Dog Training Center in Fort Royal, Virginia, on the 20th of October, 1945, to be retrained. He needed to learn to be a civilian again. He was taught to trust more people than just his handlers, to know that people were friendly -- and not lunge when he thought someone was going for his gun. He was taken into town to become accustomed to cars and bikes whizzing by. And noise, he had become accustomed to alerting his handler for tiny noises in the no man's land; now he had to let the noises go. Before being release, his health was also Okayed by a veterinarian.

Chips was discharged from the War Dog Detachment of the U.S. Army Quartermaster Corps on 10 December 1945.

Chips was sent by train at the Army's expense back to Pleasantville New York and the Wren family. The New York Central train arrived at 9:30 a.m. on December 11. The Wren's two older daughters had to stay in school so Mr. & Mrs. Wren and their four-year-old son, Johnny, met the train with a small gathering of adults. They waited for the boxcar door to open. Expecting to see Chips, six newsmen and photographers crowded the door and got out – they had been riding with the dog. Then Chips was moved to the front in his large wooden crate with a wire mesh window. After a few photos, the Wrens led Chips to the car and took him home. Later that day there were reunions with the rest of the family and neighbors. Then he slept the rest of the day.

Later, when asked whether they noticed any changes in Chips, Mr. Wren said, "He doesn't seem to wag his tail as much as he did before going to war, but I suppose he is suffering from battle fatigue."

Some sources have said Chips was returned to his handler after coming home, but he was living with his family at the time of his death, which doesn't support this.

Chips broke his tail falling from a military truck in Italy. It's believed he injured his kidneys then. Later he developed serious kidney disease and died of it on April 17, 1946. He was six years old and had been home with the Wrens just four months.

Chips was buried at the Hartsdale Pet Cemetery, in Hartsdale, New York.

The Medal Uproar

When Chips was awarded his medals for his valor there was much press coverage. Now, it was the policy of the military not to give medals to animals, but most were willing to let this slide for Chips. Some people, however, thought it demeaned the human winners of the award by also giving them to a dog. The most effective of the complainers was William Thomas, national commander of the Military Order of the Purple Heart. He took his complaint to the president and to the secretary of war. Newspaper comments at the time reported that the medals had been revoked in early 1944. After that, it was time for dog lovers to be upset.

When Chips was being discharged, members of his platoon gave him their own awards – a Theater Ribbon with the arrowhead for his assault landings and battle stars for his eight "theaters" that he fought in. These awards were not official but showed how much these weary soldiers thought of Chips. They'd also giving him several Purple Hearts of their own earlier to decorate his collar.

It seems, however, that Chips kept at least his silver medal for valor. His owner, Mr. Wren, was quoted by the New York Times in December, 1945, as saying the Army said he could keep the Silver Star but that they were revoking the Distinguished Service Medal. No mention was made of the Purple Heart; this may have been revoked as well to assuage Thomas. Over a million awards for the Purple Heart were issued; Chips is not on any of the lists but none of the lists are complete.

In a list of Silver Star recipients, Chips is listed as A. Chips, HQ, 3d Infantry division GO No. 79 (1943).

Winkie, Chinka, Mickey and Etta & Kitty

Every war has its dog heroes – their actions have been incredible. But there is another type of war dog: the civilian dogs whose comfy lives of walks and treats are shattered by war.

Paris has always been the most dog-loving city of the world. Winkie, Chinka, and Mickey were living in Paris at the beginning of World War II. They were tiny dogs, probably French poodles. They were walked on one leash that split into three at the very end so they walked side by side and didn't stray. They vacationed on the Riviera and sat under restaurant tables all over France accepting goodies.

They lived in the center of Paris on the sixth floor of a modern twelve-floor apartment house. The apartment had five rooms and a bath. Winkie, Chinka, and Mickey lived with three women. Etta Shiber, Kitty Beaurepos and their maid, Margot. The dogs knew the apartment concierge, Madame Beugler, very well as she was very friendly with the dogs and the women.

Etta Shiber had been a housewife in Manhattan with interests in art and music; her husband was a wire services chief at a New York newspaper. Etta had been to Paris several times. At first she'd come with her husband. In 1925, she found a little dress shop that made clothing that she liked and she got to know and like the lady who owned it, Kitty. They became friends. Etta came back to Paris almost every year after that.

In 1933, Etta came to Paris with her brother, Irving, for his health. Instead of getting better he became seriously ill there. Frantic, Etta went to Kitty for help. Kitty found good doctors but Irving died. Kitty then helped with the funeral and arranged the burial. Kitty even stayed with Etta at her hotel.

Three years later, Etta's husband, William, died. She cabled her sadness to Kitty who promptly invited Etta to come live in Paris with her. Etta arrived in Paris barely a week later.

Kitty was from a wealthy family in England. She married an Italian who passed away. Later she married a French wine merchant. They didn't divorce, but stopped living in the same apartment. She and Henri had a strange but loving relationship. Kitty opened the dress shop out of boredom, not because she needed the money.

The apartment was crammed with furniture, art, and knickknacks the two women had brought from their former homes. And when they were living there they added even more. The dogs had plenty of places to hide and play but their humans were rather cramped.

A little history

When Germany invaded Poland on September 1, 1939, France and Britain declared war on Germany two days later. Nothing much happened during what was called the "Quiet War" until May 20, 1940, when Germany invaded France and Belgium. The French, British, and Belgium forces were quickly overcome. They were pushed to the Atlantic Coast where 338,000 were evacuated by military and civilian craft of all kinds from Dunkirk, France. Thousands of other British and French soldiers missed the Dunkirk boats and were marooned in France; many were captured but some managed to escape via underground activities in France.

On June 13, 1940, German troops entered Paris unopposed. Later, on June 22, France and Germany signed an armistice. The terms of the armistice were that Germany would occupy the Atlantic coast of France and the north. An unoccupied zone was established in the south of France under the French government which had fled from Paris to Vichy.

June 13, 1940: Nazis Come to Paris

Etta and Kitty did not realize until too late that most people had left Paris -- especially the British, who were still fighting the Germans and would be considered enemies.

On June 13, the streets were empty and eerily quiet when they called their embassies and found their governments had deserted the city. Kitty rushed off to get her car while Etta fumbled about trying to figure out what to take with them. Kitty had to do the packing when she returned and they rushed to the car. The car was a convertible and the back seat was piled high with their cases. The dogs sat in front on the women's laps.

At first, there was no traffic, but soon they met the hordes trying to flee south. For over a day they crept forward a foot or so at a time. Finally, Kitty took a side road and was able to drive quite fast. Shortly, however, they met autos coming from the other direction fleeing the Germans. They turned around and followed them. Not long after, as they were approaching the main road again, airplanes swooped down and machine-gunned people and animals along the road. The trembling dogs,

Kitty, and Etta cowered in a ditch until the planes finally stopped.

German soldiers then crowed onto the road and they were commanded to return to Paris. The way to the south was blocked.

The Adventure Begins in Ernest

On the way back they stopped at an inn. The proprietor told them that he was out of food – didn't even have sugar for their tea – but they forced their way in. Kitty charmed him into offering tea (with sugar), bread, and cheese. When he heard them speaking English he asked for help. There was a British airman, William Gray, hiding at the Inn who had been left behind at Dunkirk and wanted to get back in the fight. Gray had wanted to buy some civilian clothes and the innkeeper was having trouble making him understand: if he kept his uniform on and was captured he'd be sent to prison – in civilian clothes he'd be shot immediately.

Loyal to her British roots, Kitty wanted to help despite the danger of her being executed herself by the Germans. The car had a luggage space tucked behind of the back seat. Gray crawled in there and off they went. They were stopped several times during the trip back to Paris, but no one searched the hidden luggage compartment.

They sneaked William into the apartment. And then the fear began. The Germans were going systematically block by block checking the resident lists against those they found. The dogs barked whenever anyone came near the door, but the women never did devise a plan. So one day, German officials knocked at the door. Kitty went to the door as slowly as she could but had to let them in. They searched room by room. Etta was in her bedroom with William. There was nowhere to hide, getting under the bed would've been silly. Her eyes lit on a photo of her brother Irving – back at the inn, she'd been taken by William's resemblance to her brother. Within seconds she had William undress, get into bed, and she placed a wet cloth over his forehead.

The Germans bought the story Etta told of her brother's being sick and staying with them to recover. She had her brother's papers. One of the Germans even added her brother's name to the apartment's list of allowed occupants.

Later, the women found an underground route for William to escape to the south. This route quickly evaporated. During this time many of the French collaborated with the Germans and betrayed the underground. Later, anger at food shortages and the many restrictions on their lives more French resisted where they could. They were even forbidden to gather in cellars during allied bombing because the Germans couldn't monitor all the meetings.

Saving Men

Kitty and Etta didn't stop with William Gray. They next rescued two British airmen from a hospital. In trying to find a way for them to escape they connected with Father Christian, who had established a wide network leading to the south. There were a thousand of the soldiers living in nearby woods. Almost every day they'd leave a body for Father Christian to bury. The women and the priest quickly fell into a routine. The priest would bring four men to the apartment and the women would ferry them to the train or to another stop in the underground. Before they were stopped they rescued at least 150 men together.

During these scary months the dogs did more that alert them of people near the door. Their attachment to them lessened the everyday grinding anxiety about being caught.

The women joined the Foyer du Soldat, a welfare agency to support the French troops. The Germans used the agency to deliver packages to prisoners in the hospitals in the occupied areas. As a member, Kitty was able to get gas for the car. One reason the Germans allowed this was they had a shortage of transport. Germans were going from house to house and clearing the valuables from any place not being lived in. Trucks and trains were needed to take the spoils back to Germany.

On November 26, five months after they had stuffed William Gray in the luggage compartment and just after celebrating the 150th saved man, Kitty was in the South of France getting more money for bribes, fuel, and food for the men. Etta was alone with the dogs in the apartment. Margot had left early to stand in line to buy food, something that took half her days.

The bell rang. Thinking it was Father Christian with four more British soldiers, she opened the door. It was the German police. She was ordered to pack a few things and leave with them. They left one man in the apartment to arrest Kitty and monitor the telephones.

Etta stopped as they were leaving the apartment and said that she had to tell the concierge to take care of the dogs. With this ploy she managed to whisper to Mme. Beugler what was happening and for her to warn Father Christian not to go up to the apartment.

Etta was questioned for hours but denied knowing where Kitty was or anything about her activities. They brought her to a famous military prison that just two years before Etta and Kitty had visited as tourists. Strip searched, photographed, and given a number, she was shoved into a stinking cell with four cots. It was so crowded there was no space to pace. Every day the four women sat on the edge of their cots waiting the days away. Finally, on December 14, Etta was released.

Returning to the apartment she met happily with her excited dogs. Kitty was still away but everyone else involved with their underground activity had been arrested. Margot had been released and she left Paris for her family home.

Later, Etta met with Kitty's husband, Henri, who convinced her to leave Paris for the South. Etta was being used by the Nazis as bait to catch Kitty. So Etta and Henri devised a plan for the following day to trick her followers and reach the train station.

December 22, the day she was planning to escape, Etta decided to take the dogs for one last walk. She put them on the leash and headed for the elevator which was already rising. Out came the same German who had arrested her before. He said she was wanted at headquarters.

Excited about going for a walk, Winkie, Chinka, and Mickey whined as she took them off the leash and closed the door behind them. Hoping for a bureaucratic snafu, Etta found out at headquarters that they had arrested Kitty and she was going to be held as a witness.

On March 7, 1941, there was a trial. The jury were six privates of the German army. They were all found guilty. Kitty and Father Christian were sentenced to death. Etta was sentenced to three years hard labor; her sentence was lighter as the United States was not in the war yet. Others had longer sentences.

Etta was in three different prisons over 17 months. Hard labor for her, as she was in her 60s, meant she was not allowed to go outside for the two hours each day the others were given in the first prison. Food was scarce and awful, the prisons cold. She had several heart attacks. Then, after her last heart attack, she was told she was being paroled. She could return to Paris but would need to report to the Germans each day. She discovered they released her from prison because they wanted to exchange her for a German woman convicted of espionage in the United States. They were afraid that Etta might die if they kept her in prison any longer.

Civilian casualties

So weak she couldn't walk the two miles to the train station, Etta made her way back to Paris. Close to home she grew excited to see her dogs again. She hardly recognized Mme. Beugler, the concierge, she had become so thin. Etta looked for her dogs ... but they weren't there. Mme. Beugler explained that with the food shortage in Paris all the dogs in the city had been eaten – and many cats as well.

Etta was horrified. But somewhat relieved when the concierge went on to explain that she didn't have enough food to feed the dogs so had them put to sleep. She hadn't eaten the dogs. Or so she said.

Little Winkie, Chinka, and Mickey were gone, casualties of the war.

The Endings

Etta's apartment had been taken over by the Germans. First, they had taken everything out and trucked it away. Then they brought everything back so the German who'd first come to arrest her could live there.

Kitty was in prison in France for some time but was then transferred to Germany. It was assumed she died there or was executed. It was sad. Kitty had been tricked by the Gestapo into a confession which had also implicated Etta. They showed her a fake confession of Etta's but Etta never confessed anything.

Father Christian was scheduled to be killed. On the day of his execution, two officers appeared at the prison to take him away. Later, two real officers appeared to take him away and discovered they'd been tricked. British supporters of Father Christian had rescued him and he went deep underground to continue his work.

Etta returned to the United States. She wrote a book of her adventures, *Paris Underground*, which was made into an awful movie in 1945. She died in 1948 at the age of 70 from complications of a broken hip.

Barry and the Monks

Barry was dog who lived with monks at an inn and monastery at the St. Bernard Pass in Switzerland. Barry was credited with saving at least 40 people lost or trapped by avalanches in the Alps.

The monks

There was a long, approximately 50-mile route passing through the Alps that connected the valleys of Aosta, Italy and Martigny, Switzerland. The pass was between Mount Blanc and Mount Rosa and was used by villagers, travelers, warring tribes, and armies through history.

The pass saw some important historic characters, included Caesar. This was the route Napoleon took in 1800 to attach the Austrian army – legend has it that he slid down the Italian side on the seat of his pants.

The route was difficult and dangerous. Except for a few summer months, the pass was covered in snow seven or eight feet deep with drifts five times higher. Steep mountains along the pass combined with the massive snowfalls to create frequent avalanches which often buried those trying to pass along the way. Then, there were wolves. And maybe even worse, bandits lived in caves and waylaid travelers, robbing and killing them.

Bernard of Menthon (sometimes called Bernard of Montjoux) had come from a wealthy family which had its roots in France but was in Geneva during Bernard's time. Bernard was supposed to marry but escaped his family to join the Augustine order in Aosta. Concerned by the dangers of the pass, he proposed that the Augustines build an inn (called a hospice) and a monastery for travelers' safety at the highest point of the pass at 8000 feet. This was established around 1050 and still exists today. Thought to be a holy man within the Alpine region, Bernard was canonized by Pope Innocent XI in 1681, Pope Pious XI confirmed him as the patron saint of mountain climbers in 1923.

The dogs

It is thought that the first dogs at the monastery arrived in the mid-1600s. They were first there to protect the monks against wolves and bandits and were the type of dog popular with the area's farmers. In the 1700s, servants from the hospice often took travelers down to Martigny on the Swiss side of the Alps. About 1750, the servants began to take dogs with them when they guided people. The more they were with the dogs, the more they valued their talents, especially their sense of smell. If fogged in, the dogs could find their way back to the hospice. They could find people buried in avalanches many feet deep. And if several dogs led the servants, the dogs' wide chests and big feet could plow a path for them to follow.

After some time, the monks started sending two or three dogs out together without a human to look for people lost on the pass. It became a routine for the dogs. They'd find the lost people, often digging through snow. Then they'd lick them into consciousness and guide them back to the hospice. If the person couldn't walk, one of the dogs would lie on top of him while the other dogs would go back to get help.

Over more than two hundred years the dogs are credited with saving 2000 lives. The monks and servants never trained the dogs – they trained each other, with the puppies following the larger dogs.

Barry, history and legend

Barry was born in 1800. He was credited with saving at least 40 people on the pass and had become famous during his lifetime. While the hospice kept no records for individual dogs, most researchers believe that he did save that many people because he was so revered at the hospice. After Barry's death, they always named another of their dogs Barry.

Much of what's "known" and written about Barry is pure fable. Some of the "facts" about Barry involve the brandy cask, the child on his back, and his death:

The cask

Maybe the most famous non-truth about Barry and the other hospice dogs is that they carried casks around their necks filled with brandy or another alcoholic beverage to revive the fallen traveler. But the dogs *never never* carried a cask or liquor. Some of the dogs may have carried small packs on their backs, but never a cask.

When Barry died, his skin was preserved, stuffed, and put on display at the Museum of Natural History in Berne, Switzerland. The original model had a cask around his neck. Since then some of the museum directors have taken the cask off, others keep it on. It's on now.

The child on his back

Barry was said to have gone to find a boy trapped on an ice shelf. Barry's nose found the child, his tongue licked him to life, and his body lay on the boy to keep him warm. After waiting and no humans came to the rescue, Barry managed to get the child on his back and take him to safety at the hospice.

This tale was told about other hospice dogs before Barry was even born. Despite this, it's often told as fact. While it can be believe that the dog could have guided a child back, putting him on his back and carrying him down the mountain isn't thought possible.

The legend persists. Famous etchings of the deed have been published. The story is even written on a monument erected in 1900 honoring Barry in the famous dog cemetery in Paris, the Cimetière des Chiens.

Clichy - Asnières — Le Cimetière des chiens

Barry's tragic death

It is said that when Barry went to rescue his 41st victim, he found an unconscious Swiss soldier. When the dog licked his face, the soldier came to and stabbed Barry in the side, thinking he was being attacked by a wolf. Barry, wounded, still managed to crawl back to the hospice and alert the monks to save the soldier.

In fact, Barry worked on the mountain until 1812 when he was taken by a prior to live in Berne. He died there in 1814.

The Newfies

Why did Barry become so famous if so many of his exploits weren't true? First of all, he was a wonderful rescue dog. But soon after his death there was a period of terrible avalanches that killed most of the hospice dogs. Barry was really one of the last of his breed, and all the exploits and legends of the breed were given to him.

Thinking it would help survival of future dogs, the hospice bred the original dog with Newfoundlands, thinking the Newfies' long hair would help keep the dogs warmer. What happened was that the long hair was a disaster – the hair froze and made the dogs even more susceptible to the cold. Barry was really one of the last of his breed. While some of the original dogs remained, they were bred with other breeds to create today's St. Bernard dog.

The St. Bernard

The hospice dogs weren't called St. Bernard's until the Swiss Kennel Club established the breed in 1880. The past and present breed of St. Bernard's is much different from Barry. Even the current stuffed Barry had cosmetic surgery in 1923. The skin had fallen into pieces. But during the procedure, Barry's head was made bigger in an attempt to make him appear more like the St. Bernards of that time. And even since 1923 the breed continued to change. If Barry were put side by side with a modern St. Bernard you would not think they were the same breed.

Barry weighed somewhere between 90 and 100 pounds; modern St. Bernards weigh between 140 and 190 pounds. Barry had longer legs, shorter hair, and a longer tail. And Barry did not have that huge jowly face and shaggy hair we associate with St. Bernards today.

Much has been written about the breeds of dogs that created today's St. Bernard. Most today accept that the monks started with the local farmer dog, or Sennenhunds. The Sennenhunds are thought to have come from the time the Romans were in the area. These dogs had a red-brown coat similar to Barry's. Then breeds most often suggested to have been crossed with the local dog in the 1800s include the Alpine Spaniel, Pyrenean Mountain Dog, Leonberger, Newfoundland, many Mastiff breeds.

The Modern St. Bernard

The stuffed Barry after 1923 cosmetic surgery

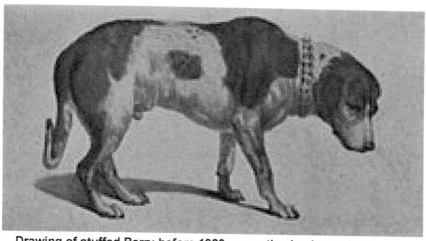

Drawing of stuffed Barry before 1923 cosmetics by James Watson book

The Hospice and its dogs today

Time passed. In addition to the changing face of the dogs themselves, other changes were made at the hospice. The building during Barry's time was constructed in 1560. A newer building was added in 1898. The following year, the monks built a hotel. The hotel was opposite the hospice on the same site but is in Italy, not Switzerland. The monks hired a separate company to provide the hotel services while they continued offering more sparse lodging for travelers.

A carriage road was constructed over the pass in1906 passing between the hospice buildings. Year later, a paved road was constructed that skirts by the buildings; it's the third-highest road in Switzerland.

There are now two lives at the hospice. From June to mid-October, large tour buses stop, the tiny hotel is open – it has 27 family rooms -- and there's a definite touristy vibe to the area. But during the remaining months Nature prevails. The road is closed, the hotel is closed. The hospice remains open and accessible to the hardy souls who come by ski and snowshoe.

The monks are still there, though just a few are there full-time. The monastery provides respite for other monks.

What about the dogs? St. Bernard dogs are no longer used for rescue. The area now uses helicopters and heat sensors to find people lost or buried in snow. The St. Bernard is too heavy a dog to lower to rescue sites from the air.

The hospice continued to house dogs at the mountain site until 2004, when the upkeep of the dogs and the building were too much for the monks. The dogs were sold to a charitable group, Barry Foundation, which keeps the dogs during the winter at their museum in Martigny, and brings some of them up to the hospice in summer. To pay for their keep, tourists can schedule walks with the dogs year-round. (A 1½ hour walk costs almost $50 for an adult.)

Stubby and Convoy

America entered World War One in April 1917. In July of that year, a mongrel dog – a bull terrier-type – wandered the streets eating from the garbage pails of New Haven, Connecticut. The dog had a sturdy solid body connected to a small head, stub tail, and short legs. One day he appeared on the Yale parade ground where an infantry regiment was undergoing basic training before being sent to the war. Their barracks were nearby. The camp was close to where the Yale Bowl currently sits.

The soldiers on the field were members of the 102nd Regiment, 26th Infantry Division. The regiment was made from two divisions that were incomplete, the 1st and 2nd Connecticut Divisions. So the army put a '0' between the one and the two and came up with the 102nd as the name for the new Regiment.

The dog kept coming back. One of the soldiers, John Robert Conroy, liked the dog and started slipping him some food. Others followed suit. Soon the dog was sleeping in the barracks with them. Conroy picked the name "Stubby" for the stub of a tail that he tried to wag so vigorously.

Stubby was born for the military. He learned what the different bugle calls were for. He managed to stay with them when they practiced marching quick changes of direction. They even trained him to salute.

In September or October 1917, the unit went to Newport News Virginia and Conroy sneaked Stubby onto the train under his long army coat. He did the same thing to get Stubby on board the ship that was taking them to France.

At this point the story has conflicting legends. One is that Conroy hid Stubby in a coal bin and that when he was discovered he saluted and melted the hearts of those who found him. The other rendition is that Conroy was with Stubby when some officers discovered the dog. Conroy spoke out "Present Arms!" and Stubby saluted. Whatever the story, Stubby was detected but allowed to remain on board. His effect on the soldiers' morale quickly earned him a permanent place as the regiment's dog.

War Dogs

Men have probably always used dogs to gain an upper hand in their disputes. Before gunpowder was invented, the dogs themselves were the weapon. Packs of dogs were trained to attack.

Germany used about 30,000 dogs in World War One, the allies close to 25,000. Unlike its allies, the United States had trained no dogs for war. The US paid for some sentry and messenger dogs trained by the allies.

Dogs were particularly useful in the trench warfare. By the end of the war, there had been at least 24,000 miles of trenches dug.

Their superior senses of smell, sight, and hearing made dogs ideal for sentry and scouting duties. The sentry dogs stayed with one handler and magnified the power of a sentry. Scout dogs went with small patrols; these were silent dogs, trained to point to alert the patrol of danger.

Messenger dogs were used to deliver messages between the different lines of trenches or back to their command control. They ran faster than a man could and were lower and less noisy.

The Germans more than any others trained dogs to go into no-man's-land at a time too dangerous for the men. The dogs would seek out the wounded and carried saddle packs with medicines. These dogs would also stay and comfort the dying.

Any of the dogs used in the trenches could also double as mascots. Just having a dog around could comfort the men.

Stubby in France

America had come to the war underprepared. When Stubby's company reached France they were put with experienced French forces for training in trench warfare. The French were not at first impressed by their allies but the Yanks learned quickly.

The regiment's men became fierce fighters. A case in point: one day a force of Germans much larger than they crept upon them in a town. The cooks were the first to detect them. One cook delayed their attack by swamping them with boiling water. Another cook attacked with his cleaver and killed two of the enemy. The Americans won that fight.

Stubby's war began in early February 1918. The loud noise of war was ever present. Noise bothers a lot of dogs, leading to whining and burrowing for relief. The war noises infuriated Stubby – he howled in rage when each round of shooting started.

After being gassed once and learning about the chemical first hand, the next time Stubby detected a mere sniff of it he tore around the trenches waking his men, even biting them, to get them to put their gas masks on. Stubby's face wasn't a good shape for gas masks so after he alerted the men he buried his face until the gas lifted.

Stubby in his greatcoat

Stubby could also hear better than the soldiers, so alerted the men when an artillery shell was coming their way. And, after a while, he could even detect when the Germans were coming out of their trenches to attack. Stubby's intelligence grew. He learned to tell the difference between allied and German uniforms. And he could tell whether English or German was being spoken.

When the allies were marching German prisoners of war near Stubby they had to tie him back – he wanted to tear them apart.

In April, 1918, Stubby was badly wounded in his chest and leg by shrapnel from a hand grenade which landed him in a Red Cross Hospital. When recovering, he went about cheering up the men before he went back to the front. At this time he began to hide from the noise of the big guns – but came right back on duty when they stopped.

In addition to his duties in the trenches, Stubby also ventured into no-man's-land to help his wounded. If the man could walk, he led him back. If he needed assistance, Stubby would stay and bark until someone came. If he were dying, Stubby stayed with him.

After one battle, the women of the town made Stubby a chamois shirt embroidered with the flags of the allied countries. As Stubby earned his medals and chevrons, they were added to his shirt.

The Argonne

The battle of the Argonne Forest was the final campaign of the war fought along a huge front. Stubby was busy with his duties when he heard someone in what had been an unoccupied section of his trenches. When he went to investigate, he surprised a German spy who had come to map the area. The spy made a mistake – he attempted to calm Stubby down by speaking to him. He spoke to him in German and Stubby attacked. Stubby nipped him and the spy left the trench and ran for it. Stubby leapt and got a firm bite of his backside, brought the spy down and kept him there until his men came.

The spy wore a medal called the Iron Cross. The men pinned it onto Stubby's coat for his reward. Later the medal was lost. Stubby's commander nominated him for promotion from corporal to sergeant for his bravery.

Sergeant Stubby

After that event, Stubby was gassed several more times. But fortunately, Stubby survived the war. He enjoyed a long stay in France waiting for a trip home. He even got to shake hands with President Wilson. Finally, Conroy took Stubby on board a troop ship again, perhaps less furtively this time.

Back home

Stubby had fought in 17 battles in four major campaigns: Aisne-Marne, Champagne-Marne, St. Mihiel, and Meuse-Argonne. Stubby returned home in the spring of lots of attention. He marched in parades, leading many of them, and continued to make public appearances until he died. The press loved Stubby -- even the New York Times reported on Stubby – his medal from Pershing, his death, and the recovery in 1931 of a lost painting of him.

Stubby was made a member of the American Red Cross, the YMCA, and the American Legion. He was elected Hero Dog at a Boston dog show. In 1921, there was a ceremony to honor veterans of Stubby's regiment. As part of the ceremony, Stubby was given a medal by his former commander-in-chief General John J. Pershing. Solid gold, etched with a simple "Stubby", the Hero Dog medal was provided by the precursor of the Humane Society. Pershing pinned the medal on Stubby's chamois shirt after giving a speech praising his bravery.

Stubby was welcome everywhere – from posh hotels to the White House. He met three presidents: Woodrow Wilson, Calvin Coolidge, and Warren G. Harding

Robert Conroy kept Stubby and took the dog with him when he went to Georgetown to study law. The dog, now famous, became the college mascot – amusing the fans at halftime with his antics with a football.

After college, Conroy worked for several federal intelligence agencies and for a Connecticut congressman. Stubby died in his arms on March 16, 1926. Conroy had the dog's skin mounted by a taxidermist, with Stubby's ashes inside the form. In 1956, he donated Stubby complete with his coat, medals, and a scrapbook of press clippings to the Smithsonian National Museum of American History.

Among his medals, Stubby was awarded The Victory Medal, the Purple Heart, the Republic of France Grande War Medal and the Medal of Verdun.

Afterword

The dogs in this book helped their humans quite differently. While some performed heroic actions during wartime, others supported their humans with their simple cheerful presence. What amazed me was how much of what they did wasn't from being trained to do it. They instinctively knew what was needed of them.

The dogs at St. Bernard Pass, not the monks, trained their pups to rescue travelers. And if, like Almo, they were trained in specific abilities – they still went far beyond their training using their own brains and hearts to support their humans. Chips even went *against* his training to protect his men.

Almost every day we read of some unusual feat a dog has done. As I was writing this I Googled "dog saves" ... and today it was a baby porpoise caught in the rocks. Some days it's a dog jumping in front of a car to save a baby.

I just hope we deserve our dogs.

Sources

Balto and Seppala

Wikipedia. *Gunnar Kaasen.*
https://en.wikipedia.org/wiki/Gunnar_Kaasen

Earl J. Aversano. *Balto's True Story*
http://www.baltostruestory.net/serumrunsynopsis.htm

Seaman and Meriwether Lewis

The Journals of the Lewis and Clark Expedition.
http://lewisandclarkjournals.unl.edu/   This site has day-by-day text
of journals of both Lewis and Clark

Wikipedia. *The Timeline of the Lewis and Clark* Expedition
en.wikipedia.org/wiki/Timeline_of_the_Lewis_and_Clark_Expedition

Wikipedia. *Meriwether Lewis.*
en.wikipedia.org/wiki/Meriwether_Lewis

Charles B. Greenberg, Ph.D. *Pittsburgh as Frontier Gateway in
1803 and Staging Point for The Lewis & Clark Expedition (1-4),*
http://www.ic.pitt.edu/Pittsburgh_Legacy_Lewis_and_Clark

Fort Mandan Foundation *Discovering Lewis & Clark®* www.lewis-
clark.org This site has photos taken from the air to illustrate the
terrain the expedition was following; with photos are maps and
descriptions of each leg of the expedition as well as changes in
geography since, from dam construction etc.

National Park Service. *Seaman.*
http://www.nps.gov/jeff/learn/historyculture/seaman.htm

PBS website. *Inside the Corps, Seaman*
http://www.pbs.org/lewisandclark

Kate Kelly. *Seaman, A Newfoundland Dog Who Accompanied Lewis and Clark*
http://americacomesalive.com

James J. Holmberg. Seaman's Fate? *We Proceed On*, 7-9, Vol. 26, No. 1, Feb. 2000.
http://www.lewisandclark.org/wpo/issue_index.php

Almo and Christensen

W.A. Christensen. Almo - *"His Master's Eyes"*. DeVorss & Co., Los Angeles, 1935. (Note, this book can be read online at http://www.hathitrust.org)

Pioneer Seeing Eye Dog Is Preserved. Popular Science, September 1940.

Lasse and Amundsen

Roald Amundsen. *The South Pole (Volumes I & II)*. Translated from the Norwegian by A.G. Chater. John Murray, London, and Lee Keedwick, New York. 1913.

Stein Tronstad and Ted Scambos. *Historic Names*. From website of Norwegian-U.S. Scientific Traverse of East Antarctica, 2009 expedition. traverse.npolar.no/historical-traverses/historic-names

Website, SouthPole.com

Website for Polarship Fram. www.fram.nl/faq/name/polarship.htm

Sarah's Dogs website. *Greenland Dog*
www.sarahsdogs.com/breeds/greenland-dog

Wikipedia. *Roald Amundsen and Amundsen's South Pole Expedition*. en.wikipedia.org/wiki/Roald Amundsen

Bothy with Ranulph & Virginia Fiennes

Ranulph Fiennes. *To the Ends of the Earth.* Simon & Schuster UK; September 2014

Sir Ranulph Fiennes and Virginia Fiennes. *Bothie the Polar Dog.* Hodder & Stoughton Ltd, UK, 1984

The Guardian. **Virginia Fiennes:** *Feisty explorer who masterminded her husband's polar treks. Monday 23 February 2004 21.35 EST.*

http://www.theguardian.com/news/2004/feb/24/guardianobituaries.gender

Dogs through History website.
http://homepage.ntlworld.com/k.westgate/history.htm

Transglobe Team in Antarctic: A News Bulletin.
http://www.antarctic.org.nz/pdf/Antarctic/Antarctic.V9.5.1981.pdf

Transglobe Expedition Website. *Charlie Burton* (1943-2002) and *Virginia Fiennes* (1947-2004)
http://www.transglobe-expedition.org/page/update

Wikipedia. *Transglobe Expedition*
https://en.wikipedia.org/wiki/Transglobe_Expedition

Chips and the Wrens

New York Times. *Dog Hero is Dead.* April 19, 1946

Anna M. Waller. *Dogs and National Defense: Study on the history of War Dog training and utilization during and after World War II.* Department of the Army/
Office of the Quartermaster General. 1958.
www.qmfound.com/War_Dogs.htm

New York Times. *Chips, Dog Hero of the Invasion of Sicily, Receives Big Welcome on Return Home.* December 12, 1945.

Olive Drab. *WW II K-9 Chips.* olive-drab.com › War Dogs › Famous

Dwight Jon Zimmerman. *Chips: War Dog Hero of the 3rd Infantry Division.* April 12, 2014. www.defensemedianetwork.com/.../chips-war-dog-hero-of-the-3rd-infantry-division ...

Kate Kelly. *Chips, First Dog Sent Overseas in World War II.* americacomesalive.com/.../**chips**-first-**dog**-sent-overseas-in-world-war-ii/

Sandra Estrada. *Chips: Decorated War Hero.* www.military.com/NewContent/0,13190,K9_051605,00.html

Winkie, Chinka, Mickey and Etta & Kitty

Etta Shiber with Anne and Paul Dupre. *Paris Underground.* Charles Scribner's Sons, New York, 1943.

Karen Abbott. *"I Was Looking Forward to a Quiet Old Age"* Smithsonian.com. May 25, 2012. http://blogs.smithsonianmag.com/history/files/2012/05/

New York Times. *Obituary: Mrs. Shiber Dies; Nazi Foe in War.* Dec. 25, 1948.

Barry and the Monks

Jess Blumberg. *Barry and the Monks of St. Bernard.* Smithsonian Magazine, Jan. 2008. www.smithsonianmag.com/.../a-brief-history-of-the-st-bernard..

Reading Workbook Blog. "To the Rescue" Edcon Publishing. April 18, 2010 http://readingworkbook.blogspot.com/2010/04/to-rescue-from-edcon-publishing.html

Wikipedia. *Barry (dog)* https://en.wikipedia.org/wiki/Barry_(dog)

Wikipedia. *St. Bernard (dog)*
https://en.wikipedia.org/wiki/St._Bernard_(dog)

Barry Foundation. Barry, *the Legendary St. Bernard* Dog http://fondation-barry.ch/en

Stubby and Convoy

BBC Schools World War One. *Sergeant Stubby*
http://www.bbc.co.uk/schools/0/ww1/25405401

Atlas Obscura. *Sergeant Stubby*
http://www.atlasobscura.com/places/sergeant-stubby

Ann Bausum. *Stubby the War Dog: The True Story of World War I's Bravest Dog.*
National Geographic Children's Books, 2014

Wikepedia. *Sergeant Stubby*
https://en.wikipedia.org/wiki/Sergeant_Stubby

The New York Times. *Portrait of Stubby Dog War Hero, Found.*
January 18, 1931

The Price of Freedom: Americans at War *Stubby*
http://amhistory.si.edu/militaryhistory/collection/object.asp?ID=15

Badass of the Week: *Sgt. Stubby*
http://www.badassoftheweek.com/sgtstubby.html

New York Times. *Stubby of A.E.F. Enters Valhalla.* April 4, 1926

Gillian Kane. *Sergeant Stubby* SLATE, May 7, 2014

Connecticut War Department. *Stubby the Military Dog*
http://www.ct.gov/mil/cwp/view.asp?a=1351&q=257892

1st Battalion - 102nd Infantry Regiment
http://www.globalsecurity.org/military/agency/army/1-102in.htm

C.N. Trueman. *Dogs In World War One*
http://www.historylearningsite.co.uk/world-war-one/the-western-
front-in-world-war-one/animals-in-world-war-one/dogs-in-world-war-
one

PBS. *The Trenches: Symbol of a Stalemate*
http://www.pbs.org/greatwar/chapters/ch1 trench.html

Photography Credits

Balto and Seppala

Balto and Gunnar Kaasan
Photo courtesy of the National Institutes of Health; Wikipedia
https://commons.wikimedia.org/wiki/File:Gunnar_Kaasen_with_Balto.jpg

Seaman and Meriwether Lewis

Portrait of Meriweter Lewis
Charles Willson Peale [Public domain], via Wikimedia Commons
https://commons.wikimedia.org/wiki/File%3AMeriweather_Lewis-Charles_Willson_Peale.jpg

Lasse and Amundsen

Amundsen and men in the hut in Antarctica. Amundsen is 5th from left.
Photo courtesy of The National Library of Norway

Oscar Wisting at the South Pole on December 14, 1911
Photo courtesy of The National Library of Norway

Chips and the Wrens
U.S. Army Photo
www.defensemedianetwork.com/.../chips-war-dog-hero-of-the-3rd-infantry-division ...

Barry and the Monks

Dog cemetery in Paris
"Dog cimetière" by desc. - arquivo do jornal francês Le Monde.fr.
Licensed under Public Domain via Wikimedia Commons -
https://commons.wikimedia.org/wiki/File:Dog_cimeti%C3%A8re.jpg#/media/File:Dog_cimeti%C3%A8re.jpg

The Stuffed Barry after 1923 cosmetic surgery
"Barry Bern" by Zenit - Own work. Licensed under CC BY-SA 3.0
via Wikimedia Commons -
https://commons.wikimedia.org/wiki/File:Barry_Bern.JPG#/media/Fil
e:Barry_Bern.JPG

Drawing of stuffed Barry before 1923 cosmetics
Drawing from James Watson book: The Dog Book (1906)
"Barry dog" by Book: James Watson - The dog book : a popular
history of the dog, with practical information as to care and
management of house, kennel, and exhibition dogs; and
descriptions of all the important breeds (1906). Licensed under
Public Domain via Wikimedia Commons -
https://commons.wikimedia.org/wiki/File:Barry_dog.jpg#/media/File:
Barry_dog.jpg

Stubby and Convoy

Stubby in his greatcoat
Wiki – public domain US because of year first published
https://upload.wikimedia.org/wikipedia/commons/9/9a/Stubby_in_his
_great_coat.jpg

"Sergeant Stubby" by Stubby: Terrier Hero of Georgetown. Licensed
under Public Domain via Wikimedia Commons -
https://commons.wikimedia.org/wiki/File:Sergeant_Stubby.jpg#/medi
a/File:Sergeant_Stubby.jpg

Printed in Great Britain
by Amazon